# Consorting the Muse in Her Upstairs Office

RALPH BOWERS

WORKBOOK PRESS LLC
187 E Warm Springs Rd,
Suite B285 Las Vegas NV 89119 USA

Website: https://workbookpress.com/
Hotline: 1-888-818-4856
Email: admin@workbookpress.com


Ordering Information:

Quantity sales. Special discounts are available on quantity purchases by corporations, associations, and others. For details, contact the publisher at the address above.


Library of Congress Control Number:

ISBN-13:        978-1-965732-64-9  Paperback Version
                978-1-965732-65-6  Digital Version


REV. DATE: 06/19/2025

# Tan

If tan dormancy be,
Then it was the colouring
Of myself before you;

But in meeting, I met pink
And was blue;
Feeling I had not reached
Deeply enough inside myself
For one as beautiful as you.

With continuation I grow red
And glow, shewing myself
Through each word said, or read;

And with commitment from amethyst
To white, as soft as the starry clime,
So sing sweet lullaby.

Your openness and warm enthusiasm
Penetrate to that zone
Wherein reign my wildest dreams.

Thou art comet tail
And meteoric shower,
And I, a simple changer
Of colour and of shade,
Lying here within the borders

Of a rose embowered glade,
But an archer's distance
From thy fleeting fancy,
Fair maid, let me by thy train –
Else how couldst
Shakespeare whisper
Exeunt?

# ARTEMIS OF ASHEVILLE

You don't need a bow,
You have your eyes;
And you don't need arrows,
You have your gazes;
So that, in your upstairs office,
With the bow of your eyes
You shoot the arrows of your gazes
Into my heart, and I feel as if I will die.

Look, you say, in your lap,
And about the chair you squirm upon,
What see you there, but flowers,
Lovely flowers?

Listen, she says,
If I am to kill you, it will be with beauty,
So you may get a good look at
What the future promises,
If only you will believe,
Believe and know,
So you may live.

# HER FAITHFUL COMPANY

The girl of the meadow has sunflower eyes
She dotes on the Sun as he glides through the sky
When the Sun disappears, head drooped, she sighs
And turns to observe the place he'll arise

She sleeps in the night, shallow and light
Awaiting the first tickling ray
Dreaming of showing him with all of her might
A devotion words fall too short to convey

The Sun knows her heart, o how it is true
And he spins golden honey to gild the sky blue
His beams her faint essences pass softly through
With Love's pure invention, the whole world to view

She's considered a Princess by all other flowers
And hers is the face whereby they measure the hours
They all are enlivened by the Sun's awesome power
And they all bear resemblances as sons and daughters

The meadow as one beneath heaven united
By the mole of the meadow goes mostly unsighted
He sleeps in the loam kept warm by the Sun
Though a herald o' the silvery Moon, he is one

He aerates the Cereus' roots in the night
That they be not banded too close nor too tight
And he visits the Four O' clocks nigh unto day
Marveling the dance of their closing at first ray

When the Sunflower Princess a-raises her head
Announcing her love with words gone unsaid
The Sun knows her heart a companion to be
And is joyously contented in her faithful company

# My Lover, Whomsoever She May Be

O, Conquistadora, I am one in need of chains to be conquested,
As I am as horrible as Achilles on the battlefield, in love;

If chains be of frilly flowers
Or Arabian scarves of silk,
Or if chains be in hope
Of engendering Mother's milk;
For what is the use
Of the middle of the road,
If it be but for a spell?
Fleeing inertia, I must move on,
A mountain for to climb,
For the movements are sublime.

Give me a maiden, a matron, a crone,
All wrapped up in one;
If she be a friend who cuts me deep,
Hapless as a lamb, a fiercesome warrior sheep,
Dirty as the devil, and yet, a spot of angel's bleach
In her heart, eternally, she will keep,
Then perhaps she is the one for me,
But the scales must lift and I must see.

If she wield a striking glance,
And, if by chance my ankle nick,
I might even die from this.
"Ah, a glorious death 'twould be",
My Conquistadora would say to me,
Whomsoever she may be.

# FLAME

She was possessed of the shape of flame,
A tapering flame, kissed by the mouth of the wind;
She illuminated my world and mirrored it in her grin,
And though I have never seen her again,
A common flame reminds me of where we had been,
When I saw her as a flame kissed by the mouth of the wind.

The stars sing lo, and the moon light soft
Glimmers on the frost of my frozen heart;
In my eyes you'll see the love we dared,
And for this love have I been spared
All loneliness unto this day.
O moving flame, don't move away.
Painting pictures of castles of gold,
Clouds in the sun as the sun sinks lo
Into the west, with my baby be,
And sing a song to her of me.

All you lovers who ever cared
To add fresh flowers to the hair
And place with hands on fingers rings,
Lift your hearts and with me sing
Of things that pass, sweet things that die
And assume their places in the sky;
And don't forget to thank the God's
For helping us put bodies on,
For without these who could tell
If it were sweet flowers that we smell
When in our lovers' tresses' we veil ourselves?

For the two into one combine
Like thoughts within the mind;
They join and reunite
And blend like day and night.

A flame she was, a flame to me
The brightest in the galaxy,
And since I know no greater truth
I share Naomi's hope for Ruth.

# WOMAN

Ah Woman,
What place hath thy grace
In the concerted corridors
Of my mind,
That an ocean's tempest
Shouldst hurl thy bark
Into the eye of the storm
Of my heart;

And there,
In some pearl enameled cave,
Render me thy knavish slave
In chains of petal and shackles of mist,
Whilst thou crown me
With thine heaven scented wing.

Jurisprudence,
Thy feet are cloudlets
Surmounting steeps of clime
To an oasis sublime,
Where golden sands and caravans
In revolutions of circuitous time
Are elliptically spun in unison
With symbols springing from a tongue
And parting lips of rhyme.

Ah Woman, but a trace
Of a smile on thy face
Is always a gladsome sign,
Telling me all is fine.

# WHAT WILL BEAUTY DO

What will beauty do
when she comes to be with you;
when she takes you by surprise
and dries your tearful eyes;
leads you by the hands
over the sands of time;
whispers in your ears
her life affirming rhyme;
what will beauty do
to make everything alright?

What wisdom will she sing
to elevate your hope;
what simple truths to teach
to help you to remain sober;
will she give you love and comfort;
will you start again anew,
chasing after butterflies
a child with no shoes;
through fields of dancing flowers
to songs of wind and bird;
will you lay you down beside her
and dream upon her word;
will you trust her with your heart
and let her heal the hurt?

What will beauty do
when she hears your soulful sighs;
what will beauty do
when like a wounded animal you cry;
what will beauty do
when you wish that you would die;
what will beauty do
to make everything alright?

# NIGHT AND DAY

Day has grown faint
And Saint Night,
Staying her fall,
Lays her abed
A pearl in a shell
Neath sea swell.

A voice from a well subtly calls,
Beckoning Night to curtain the walls
Of the crystal ball.

Night leaps from depth to brink,
Sequestering trees
 In the folds of His cape,
And river's mouths agape.

Maiden moon and her attendant stars
Shoot out from the magician's crown,
Comet and tail through the translucent façade,
Spangling Night's countenance
With mythic shapes.

"On Her eyelids how dance the flowers of Spring,"
Night reminisces and swoons.
"Thick with their perfume, Her hair," He sighs;

The stars to hear full-bloom.

# My Duchess

Although I am intimately aware of what I wish to express,
I cluck like a klutz to my Duchess,
Who giggles to herself, and yet, her smile, so fair,
On the palette of her face she's crafts there,
So as not to ruffle a feather,
Or alter the weather I brew in my attempt
To translate what I feel is heaven sent
And meant to be the bridge between us;
So that we might meet in the middle,
Above the wild and crazy river,
To circumvent the distance
On which Space is so insistent,
We stand on either shore
With our backs against the wall.

I know someday I'll reach her,
And I'll keep trying until I sweep her
Completely off her feet;
And we'll cross the prophered threshold,
Me and my precious cargo,
And undo the embargo
Space has imposed on Time
To keep the movement of my rhyme
From exciting her Philly heart,
Like a hummingbird to dart
To this sugary water urn,
And graze on the mapled grain

I have suspended in her name,
Which has been my soul solution
Since the hope of elocution
Has animated these lips
With the desire for her kiss.

# MY DANDELION

She was a dandelion and this saber tooth's meow;
The desire I have for her had arisen, I don't know how.
It's as if angels conspired to have me cross her path,
And pluck her from the meadow to place in my basket.

She was the gemstone of this man's rib cage.
While he excavated the dirt by which he is comprised,
She looked on curiously with a glitter in her eyes;
What else lay beneath that shirt to compare with her worth?

I did her an injustice if she was not my world,
Or if I had eyes for some other flower girl;
For, she was the magic stone and the one casting spells,
Nor should another name from my lips have ever fallen.

She thought she had withered and become a flower dry,
And let flow a downpour from her melancholy sky;
Her breathing became fitful, a choral wind of sighs,
While her hands of wispy florets left her stem and bade goodbye.

# MEETING

"Twas no accident we ran into one another, yesterday.
Or rather, melted, dripping wet
Into one another's presence.
And no menial slip of tongue
If I tell you,
My wish is to have a head on collision;
Make a real wreck of our meeting.

That smile of yours,
That so freely blossoms
As a flower in sun;
And as if only half hinted at,
Like a wink mistaken for a squint,
I would deign to look up from your knees
And witness laughing water tumbling
Over your earthen motherware,
 Like glaze before clay is fired,
Pooling on the work surface,
Or ground where I kneel before you,
Coiling the cherry tree trunks of your legs
And burying my head in the hollow
Of your soul engendering cave,
That I may be born all over again,
In such an ecstasy as a meeting
Of this nature is wont to yield.

# MOON KISSES

Yon moon, she came and kissed me,
As I lay snuggling 'neath my sheets,
From the tip of my tasseled crown
To the soles of my tear washed feet;
And she whispered, sleep now, sleep,
Drift along to the kingdom of dream,
Where we will continue what we started
In the play's opening scene.

I blushed, myself excited,
And 'gan to reel and swoon,
But I could not fall to sleep
Any time too soon;
The chariot o' my mind was racing
Behind her on her magic broom,
And all of the swirling Milky Way
Was gathering in my room.

I cried out, I'm bewitched,
And nay can close these eyes;
Anon, it will be morning,
And the moon, o, away she will fly;
When in the wink of a wake of sudden,
Sleepy sand from a bag of diamonds
Was sprinkled my aura o'er;
And like a petal, I slipped my seat,

Liltingly floated, a dove's feather
In the heartbeat of her undulating tide;
Until I reposed beside her,
Her arms wrapped 'round so tight,
And deep into me musing
The ivory light of her eyes did pour;
And I realized, once I awoke,
I could only ever beg more.

And now, alas, the sun's light
Washes all the world;
And lo, is this the sun's daughter
Shining here upon the floor,
Motioning me to her
With a wave of her flickering hand;
And can I resist her implore?
I who, after all, am only a mortal man …

## SOME FINE EVENING

As I gaze into the field of time
My eyes alight upon your ultimate forms,
And I intuit the beings of heaven …

Downy fawn in dreams deep forest,
Bowing timorous head in the golden dawn,
Saffron flowers, your radiant garland;
How in dandelion furze you appear to me,
As I go chasing after a butterfly-swan.

Dare I stretch my neck through the rails
For you to pet me,
Or will I shake to pieces,
Like bits of meteor entering earth's atmosphere?

Once again am I led homeward,
And I know not what or how
Christina thinks or feels,
Only imagine us aloft
In an orbit of glittering gold dust.

O, for a pitcher full of words
From the Aquarian spring
To end all Piscean longing.

Cover me in white sands
With the merciful hands
Of the Holy Ghost
Some fine evening.

## So Much So (Apollo to Daphne)

… so much so, I see morning rays bending
Upon a cozy copse, now torched aflame,
Birds are cheerily whistling your name
And teeming winds do swing tree branches high;
So that, with twilit eyes you are espied
Encurled around close twisted, aging trunks,
Waking from ceaseless night's pearl foamed revels
I wonder what a girl like you would do
Could she not break free from halls of study,
Let her wanton heart gallop through the sky,
Beseeching angels' celestial wisdom,
For, when you hear me heaving heavy sighs,
You might of your love a symbol give me,
That I gladly may retire whence I came,
And there, feel all the while, the more at home,
Who did before feel all forlorn, alone?


… so much so, I see morning rays straightening,
And where before I saw curvaceous shape,
My vision, fleet of foot, through garden gate
Attends thee, as you rise in green leaf skirt,
And bare-foot skip the long path a-wending,
A sweet tongued songbird, full trebling my name;
So that, I think my heart in kin of sun
And you, uplifted are, on rays of love,
Accomplished gymnast, balance beam dancing,
Reflected in water's waking dreaming,

A minstrel's mermaid frolicking in waves,
Blowing your conch, a multiform Triton;
And all at once you vanish, while I stay
Upon a branch, mid clear air, suspended,
As you to study make a fair retreat,
I lean back, tomorrow morning waiting.

# TEAR

I think that I should shed a tear,
But the tear it just won't come.
Some say it has frozen into a sphere
The shape of the sun.

I say it is a diamond.
You say, o know, a pearl;
So, I make of it a necklace
And give it to a girl.

She looks at me so fondly,
Then comes the soft warm smile,
And the necklace I gave is now a water stain
Which lasts but a little while.

# EAGER SOUL

Eager soul,
I see you peering through her eyes,
For, as yet, there is no apt disguise
Behind which you can be hidden;
The moment you are smitten
And take the waiting air
To meet your lover there,
Without the weight of body
Or the history that has fraught thee
With all the mortal fear
You hold so close and near;
Like the freezing to the fire
You are giving life to,
In kind with the solemn duty
To the virtue you've agreed to
In crossing the great divide.

Please know, you are espied
And deeply admired,
By one who does the same
In Love's name.

Eager soul,
I see you as immortal
Thru my aging portals,
And will be to me a friend
From now until the end;

As a beacon promoting peace
You freely give to keep;
As a charm bewitching time
Rendering it sublime;
As a rhyme on joyful lips
Bringing the hearer bliss;
As an Angel to a child
Giving her reasons to smile;
As one who gladly came
Enacting in Love's name
The precious recompense,
Supernatural innocence.

# ONE LOTUS ROSE

I walked into a garden seeking sweet repose
And overheard a lotus speaking with a rose:

Before the sun peered above the rim of the world,
While yet you slept, petals unfolded
Like the ends of fingers pressed together,
Tears dripped from the eyes of night,
As water from eaves hours after rain.

Why I, tortoise like, bide in my petaled shell
The night long, only opening at the hush
Of the sun's first soft rays, I know not;
But is it any different for lovers,
When with silken strokes you part my lips
And slip your tongue into my eager mouth?

Like a brush tip caressing a tingling canvas,
In the caves of my soul imagination traces
Primitive images on surfaces of stone;
So your touch, like the wing tip of a dove
Flutters o' er my body, and I am overwhelmed,
Yet serene and divine.

O night, night is resolved at the break of day,
As thunder claps after crooked arrows of light
Streaking through cloud veiled heaven;
So is my loneliness assuaged, when starry-eyed,
The wind brings us together and our stems enwind.

# ALL I WANT TO LIST

Sweet slumbers, I have to leave you now,
I have to leave the girl of my dreams.
The day bell brings the sun upon its wings,
The wind is skipping across the pond;
I see the daughter of the dawn
Spread her gown upon the lawn,
All things within her reach,
For their sake, are given her to keep.

I close the garden gate and wave goodbye,
I leave my feet and begin to fly
In my glittering chariot through the sky,
Seeking the destination of my work station,
Where I will spend the day whiling away
Until twilight calls my name,
And I am whisked away again to find
What I have missed in the valley of her kiss.

The velvet covers breathe
While the dream machine weaves
The scenes within my soul
Restoring me to wholeness;
In the comfort of her arms,
In her love, coal fire warm,
Her charms to me are bliss
And all I want to list.

# FOR ONE ANOTHER

Drink me in,
Hold me deep,
An eternal moment for you to keep;
Breathe my breath,
And don't forget,
I give myself without regret.

I told you no
Ten thousand times,
But, I have finally changed my mind;
So, drink and breathe,
At last relieved,
For, of my absence, you are freed.

We are one
From the very beginning,
I feel it in my soul;
We have such fun
I can't stop grinning;
As grapes fermented
Into wine,
Our bodies consecrating.

So, drink me in,
Hold me deep,
Lay beside me while we sleep;
When we awake,
We do as lovers,
We are born for one another.

# WHITE SANDS

O girl,
Seated amongst the ashes of the ocean,
You hold out your hands like scales;
The stigmata found it's way in you'
From the center of your undulating heart,
Through bonny passes, to the circumference
Of your porous skin, smelling of roses,
And soft as moon washed silk.

I have crossed divided states
To fall in awe at the wonder in your eyes,
As I have found in them chests of dreams
Yet unopened; awaiting the golden summer,
And a figure bearing keys.

Open, one by one, the petals of your heart,
Impenetrable to all, save hands of golden light
Spreading about you a finely woven skein,
Embracing you like nets of shimmering water.

Count me with your catch
And slip me into your pouch,
Sing to me the glory
Into which I am born.

And Love, carry us
Like that long-awaited wave
To the surety of a shore
Leading homeward.

# CHIVALRIC STRAINS OF CHARLEMAGNE

Peace be found in gentle streams
Brimming images of dream,
Soothe the soul and calm the sense
Warbling from the wooden fence.

Knights and steeds amongst the trees,
Beneath the feathered sounds of leaves,
Rise and put your armor on,
Bow before the golden dawn,
Pledge thy vows to kingdom come,
Raise thy swords and touch the sun,
Move to where the Spirit will,
Leaving earth from the topmost hill.

Maidens of the milk way
Hiding in the light of day,
Don your many spangled gowns,
Place your moonlit pearly crowns
Atop your blessed heads;
The twilight swirls in violet haze
Illumining the heavenly maze,
Be our guides and draw us hence
In purity and innocence.

Walking in the land of skies
Knights and maidens intertwine,
Heiros Gamos consummate

Become the arches of the gate;
Love's requited open doors
Invite the poet to explore
Age on age of God's design,
The parchment of His living rhymes.

# FAT FACED MOON

You have drunk the orange juices of the sun
And transformed them into your own milk white medium,
Much as she has taken the illuminating rays of my love
And transmuted them into the color of her hair and skin.

Milk white chocolate in eclipse,
Her eyes are dark pools in which
Her koi soul swims, invisibly.

I have laid my bamboo pole aside;
Worms wiggle from the wooden bowl,
Digging themselves holes to abide in;
Bowl good for one thing now,
Plum wine I stain my mouth with.

Before I drift to sleep, in that dim moment
Between awakened dreaming,
My lips have been kissed by a fish
And all I recall is fleeting laughter.

Radha

Many a joyous tune have I piped to thee
Radha, my love.
My glory have I sung to thee with the mouth of the wind.
Moist is the breeze wherewith I watered thy skin
And from thy body hath broken forth

Many a goodly fruit tree.
Sweet is the taste of my comfort upon thy lips,
As I warm thee with the beams of my desire,
In the day when the frost descends
From out of the storehouse of winter,
Radha, my eternal creation.

# IN THE DARKNESS OF YOUR ROOM

In the darkness of your room I wait for you,
Listening for the door to open, close.
The beat of my heart races at recognition
Of your light footfalls,
And dim sparks glow on the floorboards
As you approach.
Leaning over me your breath
Lulls like summer sun and noon,
Igniting my lifeblood quickening at your touch.

Blanket me with the shadowy branches
Of your overflowing hair,
You whose hands are flowers;
Whisper to me the buzzing
Of a bee in the wind
And fertilize my excitement.
O, I was expectant of our love
Since the day I was reborn.

Night or day I know not in your wisdom
That is lamplight to my longing
And respite from monumental despair.
May I recall this memory for an eternity
And be able to call on it at will,
So that when time severs with space
Our intimate embrace,
I can remember this moment
And bring it into the next life,
So that when we arrive again
This knowing will be known.

# The Irish Lass to Her Lover

I will show you the way to safety
If you traverse with me the wood
I will leave all of my goods
And give away my pastries
To children lining the road
Hunched over with heavy loads
Who deserve tastier treaties
In a world that is so nasty
We seek a place to flee
My lover, come away with me

Sunlight lances and dancing leaves
Rest ye here upon your knees
While I inch nearer the clearing
To see if we might cross
To the adjoining wood
Without a cost of loss
My most precious darling

And if to you I nay return
Then get yourself aside
Deep into the bracken hide
Till the wood wear night's black shawl
And then quietly crawl to the clearing
Biding close attention to your hearing
And if nothing is amiss
Dart to the adjoining forest

When you reach a trickling brook
Left then right give look
And if no one else you see
Hop the rocks that rise in the stream
And run until the first sun beam
Flames upon the meadow
Cover yourself in the field
With clusters of rosy heather
And be grateful my love
For you are at the end o' the tether

And you will sense when you are free
You will feel when you reach safety
And then my lover say a prayer
Remember when your hands were in my hair
And my lips my love you were kissing
Then go and find yourself another love
For I'd not have you miss me
Any other love above
As long as you are living

# Fire Water

We are like fire and water.
I am the son of the sun
And, of the moon, you are his daughter.
A cosmic laughter rumbles through us,
Caressing, like a wind,
The flickering flame of my tongue
And the shimmering mirror of your grin.
It has been this way in this incarnation,
And it will be this way when we both come again.

My fire will expire
And your rivers will all run dry,
But, our love will last forever,
No, our love will never die.

You purify the soul and I, the spirit.
You work at making us whole
And I work so we don't fear it;
Drawing ever nearer, till we become as one,
Aligned in the eclipse of lover's lips to lips,
And tremulous, as butterflies upon the fingertips;

Then we bow and curtsy,
And away you pirouette;
But, o my brilliant lover,
I will never forget
Shining here, all dripping wet,
My flame from orange to blue
Enfolds you like a blanket,
While you rush from your groom,
A white witch on a glittering broom.

# THE PANTHER AND THE APOLLONIAN PRINCESS

The light pours over you like cat's milk,
Licks behind your knees and into the pits of your arms;
Beads at the tips of your lashes like dew, blades of grass,
And occupies the spaces between your toes like rainwater;

Wraps you 'round like a wave tossed shawl,
And cummerbunds the coral reef of your waist;
Threads the hempen strands of your raven tresses
With winding vines of hyacinth and heliotrope;

While here, in the shadows at the forest's edge,
I am dancing with a limber willow,
In circles spinning, an awe inspired weathervane,
Neath the chocolate overhang of a leafy skein;

For, if I were to come to you,
Stealthily, like a panting panther,
Crimson tongued and salivating,
It would only be, you would scramble
To the steps of your front porch,
Throw open your creaking screen door
And run inside, to spy on me
from the sanctity of an ovoid picture window;
Leaving the light that shrouded you caving in;
Outlines falling like divining rods into a wiry tangle;

Ergo, will I remain at this distance from you,
Unbeknownst; silent and invisible as weightless air
Whispering meows only I can hear,
While you playfully bathe in the ivory light
Pouring out of the showerhead of the moon;

And when you dab yourself dry
With your terrycloth towel,
Drape it over the deck railing
And venture back in, to warm yourself
In the glow of an ancient fire,
I will unbind myself from these shadows
And, in passing, rub against your towel,
Transferring fur for moon's light,
And look quite the skunk,
Whose sunken heart, now raised,
Blazes with an ancient fire's flames,
and, I too, to my cave, retire.

# I Have Fallen

I have fallen, my love; I have fallen into a bed of green grasses.
A breath of wind from Cherubim
Hath come, my love, a creation of air
To stimulate the grasses to dance with delight,
So that I find no rest in which to sink to thee,
Ever awaiting me at the door of my bosom
With those candle lit eyes of yours,
By which you lead me over fitted boards of fir
To a mezzanine, where below
The valley in her majesty in moonlight glows,
As a mirror of myself in your embrace,
Who is budding in the beauty of your grace.

Come, my love, come up from within my frame
And let me see thy face above me,
As fingers of wind twist your flowing locks
And you fasten true forget me knots;
Bewitching and entwining forever
These two enchanted realms
With the power of your spells,
For I know your magic might,
Hath coupled day and night,
And brought together land and sea,
So that there is no seam visible
For the soul you've made immortal.

# I Can Only Ever Hope

I encountered
In teasing you,
you inclined to stomp my foot.
I would have much preferred
you gathered my lips,
A couplet
Of elegant butterfly wings
Interfused
By a dizzying sunlight,
And aspired towards
my bashful lips
in open air
With the imagination
of your own
unabashed lips;
That we might have
whetted our wings together,
Making out a melody
only butterflies effectuate.

It comes to me,
The emotional signature
I displayed
while in your presence
a year ago,
Was the same for you
as it is today;

That the girl
in me
is eternally intending
To toy
with the boy in you,
Accustomed
to such
archetypal transposition.

In opening eyes
On you anew,
I glean cornflowers from
wily ringlets
And alchemize them
in my reproductive soul,

That likes Wordsworth's
Leg shaking daffodils,
I might muse
Upon them in contemplative mood,
Whilst reposing on my placid couch.

# We Used To

The sun ran through the sky today.
It was here and gone in the blink of an eye.
The wind pulled grasses left and right
And left them lying stiff and straight,
As it closed the garden gate.
It's still and dark in the garden now.
The nightingales I hear I cannot see,
But they sing so sadly sweet, I close my eyes
And take a seat beside my heart's fire;
I see you there across the pit,
Look into your ravishing eyes
At the center of my mind's eye,
And give myself to memory.

We used to feed the river flowers
As it wound passed our cottage door,
And minnows would nibble petals
As they spun in swirling eddies;
I would hold you in my arms
And swing you off of your feet;
We danced circles in our garden complete.
We stayed the sun in the sky
And the wind would softly sigh,
The grasses twined together
Like the violins of an orchestra,
And butterflies and moths would glint like stars,
But a daydream only truly goes so far.

We used to laugh and we used to sing,
We used to give ourselves to each other;
I'd lose myself in you,
You'd lose yourself in me,
And from our solitary obsessions
We would be released.

We used to shout and we used to cry,
We used to dry one another's eyes;
I vowed I'd never let you go,
You vowed the very same to me,
And from the gaping jaws of loneliness
We would be released.

We couldn't know and neither see
How quickly Death required your company.
I woke early, nor would you rise,
And the sun ran through the sky.

# To Our Mother of the Wheat Fields

Were but I to glimpse the sun
With a child's bedazzling eyes,
My feet to idleness would run
In wheat fields of the sky;
Nor entertain a workman's thought
The lazy live-long day,
Nor to have in school been taught
T o read a write always;
But I would have nursed on nectar's light
From bells on vines that sway
The way you do when you sigh
My troubled heart away.

I was playing tag beneath the trees
And a large stone was the base,
I sought to avoid the infernal freeze
And laugh upon it safe;
Many a path were there to choose
On the left hand and the right,
And much was there to win and lose
Between the day and night;
Now halfway there I feel the load
I carry is much less,
For you have helped me pave a road
With cobbles baked of bread.

So long I've seen in quiet attired
The peace that sits and waits

Upon a flower, never to expire,
As I from my fate;
The musical silence of the choir
In the instrumental heart sings,
With the tongue of the eternal fire
Fanned of angels wings.
But whence these dreams I ask
And smile, as sure of mine own name,
Were dreamt of me when but a child
And at your call I came.

Nor can I turn back the clock
On all that time's undone,
But cast my line from this old dock
In a wheat field of the sun;
For what am I but bits of grain
My mother fashioned so,
With pearls of dew and tears of rain
And prayers she's uttered, lo;
With tasseled crown and electrum gown
I tend the threshing floor,
Gleaning memory out of sound
As they pass through the open door.

# LAMPSHADE ILLUSIONS

O, Huntress, though I have glimpsed your essence in its entirety,
For sometimes I cannot help but see clear the straightway through
And though your ravenous hounds have rent me pitiably asunder,
For the prophetic act of my open hearted blunder,
Still there is a magic magnet that's drawn me back together,
As Isis' love for Osiris, she holds out to him forever.

The butterfly, whose shimmering wings
Oftimes are so blinding,
She has thoughtfully dimmed for me,
As through the labyrinth winding
I make my way with a single thread
From a tapestry of your divining;
As I journey back from the land of the dead
And take my living place beside you.

The bones were dormant, put to no good use,
Till you bid me take them out of the closet,
And dress them with mine own true love
Who was longing to be my helpmate;
She is with me now on this ice aged earth
And she radiates the steady fire
Of the furnace of the universe
No lampshade could ever hide.

# ONE DAY LIFE

Each day I am incarnated anew
And every night I die
Sun come shining through
And moon's light hide the eyes
Naked to the sight
In darkness folded tight
As bare as any truth
That just seems right
Like a bird upon a roof
Singing to the sky

I contemplate all morning
And noon comes without a warning
I slip into a shade
While river waters bathe
A flower's tender roots
Who has taken off her boots
And loosed her petaled collar
For that she's hot all over
And as I listen to a gentle strain
The wind whispers my name

I follow through a forest
And marvel the master florist
Who dressed the winding path
To still my trembling breath
To captivate my eyes

While leaning on a staff
So far removed from thoughts of death
It might be that I've died
And I wouldn't know the difference
Between it and this short sweet life

The gorgeous sun goes setting
Deep into the west
The flower nods her head
And rests it on her breast
At the sound of the night bird's revelry
My feet begin to tap
The evening brings the end of me
And on the lap of earth I collapse
Dreaming until reveille
Awaken me mayhap

# Our Beauty Sleep

Sleeping beauties, in the night so bright,
Yet, unaware of natural moonlight,
Your slumbers, in ethereal glow,
Force up shades that come and go
Unbodied and in weightless frames,
To which we attach uncertain names,
So that we might with them converse
In an imaginative universe
Dissolving at the break of day,
When sunlight shines upon the eyes
And hides beneath a golden guise
The images faint; palpitate,
Which flit with an unnerving haste
To trees o' er hanging an unreal shore
And transform into leaves once more;
Nor can they even make a rustle
In a wind that never bustles,
For the physics of nature do not apply
In this other worldly chemistry,
And so the laws of inner space
Await till we re-enter dream's estate.

But, tis true, I must confess
I light upon you, more or less,
In vague degrees, in conscious hours,
While languishing amid the flowers
That rise above me like bold towers

Shining in the sun's gold shower;
But, when alas, I must arise,
My memory to a pygmy's height
Does barely reach up to my feet,
And if I am not too discreet
I step upon you like an ant
That makes on looking deer all pant
And wither in the sweltering heat,
As a mirage that cannot keep
The idea of an oasis
In the embrace of factual basis.

Were I to choose, you'd win hands down
To be the very juggler clown
Supporting the motions of the planets;
The upper hand of science granted
You are the force behind the big bang,
'Twas your hammer the gong clang
And in which all is enveloped;
Nor for your heart will you elope,
As the power of willy nilly notion
Is, after all, a useless potion
Against the originally seen procession
Of the endless marriage vow confession
You make nightly in the temple of dream
To your sleeping beauty kings and queens,
Whose souls you with your crowns adorn,
Announcing with your faithful horn
The immortal guests of the supper you host,
For love of us most Holy Ghost.

# THE LIGHTED LAMP

The lamp, alas, is lighted,
And it will not go out;
Nor wind, nor snow, nor rain
Will cause it the slightest strain,
Or errant thought within the brain
Have hope to win or rout;
For the lamp has been lighted in purity,
Relieved of the darkest inner doubt,
At the awakening of the impervious freedom
Only true life brings about;

And the glowing of its aura
The chosen one surrounds;
The perfect, impenetrable circle
In which the ultimate joy abounds;
And the music it makes is surely
Composed of aetherworldly sounds.

Listen, for a minute,
The voice that's thus inspired.
It exceeds the previous limit,
As the lamp's light rises higher;
So that, even the burning sun,
It takes a second seat
With the background singers of the choir,
As the lighted lamp performs successive feats
In a conflagrating of wildfire

That will not singe a leaf,
 But before which we may solemnly retire
While hearts are slowed to a mellow beat;

For the light exudes a comfort
In which we may be healed
Of the ills that have sore plagued us
While climbing up this hill,
And the demons that pursued us,
Angry dogs at tender heels,
Have been distanced and silenced,
To the point that peace is all we feel;

And the light goes on before us,
And the light is there behind,
To the undoing of oppressive gravity
And the taut parade of time,
In a space that seems as endless
As a speech of reasoned rhyme
That miraculously spells out for us,
In an alphabet sublime,
The formula of the mystery
Of the lighted lamp divine.

# O My Dove

I wanted them to love me.
I tried so hard.
 I brought my dove wings with me
And wore them like a child.
I flew and sang, the heavens rang,
And trees danced on the mountains.
I didn't have a clue
My wings would come unglue,
And I'd come crashing down.
Tears, the only sound.

I brought my heart to life,
And she smiled in their sight.
I did what I thought was right,
To win them to my side.
I accepted them completely,
My wings so softly beating.
I had dreamed about our meeting
In another life, before,
So, much to my surprise,
White feathers on the floor.

I didn't learn a lesson.
I would do it all again.
Give everything I am
To earn a trusted friend.
And o, could they rely

On my giving my best try,
Without the fear of death
Or the coffin in my breast,
To seal the buried treasure
I show them for their pleasure.

I wanted them to love me,
As much as I love myself;
That they might know the glory
Of loving someone else,
The way I love them;
Without a string attached,
And maybe that's the reason why
I undergo attack.
But, I won't take it back,
For all that they might lack.

O, my dove, I love you!
Go on ahead and fly.
I will chase right after you,
With arms raised high.
In shouting fits of laughter,
My dove, you're all that matters;
And, I'll not let you down.
But, for a million reasons,
You are the crowning achievement;
The ripeness of my season.

# If I Were a Bird

I f I were a bird, in a cool grot I would be,
To escape the heat of the world.
Soft would be the fingers of the stream
Wherewith my wing feathers were plied;
And I would ring out like a piano
Underneath the trees,
Exuding my notes
To the invisible bark of a breeze
That would ferry them into the meadow,
And drop them on the happy fellows
Cavorting in the flowers,
Withstanding the sun's awesome power;
And they would seek with eyes
Through waves of heat,
To find the place
Where I have made my seat,
But I would hide amongst the river rocks,
A ship emptied of its crew, beside a dock;
And in the shallows silent I would be
And they would not espy me.

Invisible, as voice within the mind,
In an imaginary wind, a wind chime
I would fumble, reeling with my bells;
A bare stick running
Wildly on the bars of my cell;
And I would yell out to the guard

Who bore the keys,
To come release a one
Who would be free,
And give myself in form to waiting eyes,
Naked of the mask and the disguise,
To catch them unawares and by surprise,
And leave them feeling we are very wise;
Then I'd take to wing and thither fly,
If I were a bird.

# Through the Glass Plainly

There is that thought, which many have opined,
But is false to my mind,
That it is on the fringes of mystery
One is maintained in reverie;
But I say, this is not so,
For the more I come to know you
The more deeply do I love you,
And that very accumulation of elation
Is the living mystery, lived,
Which is the ultimate reality;

As the nut in the shell itself
Differs from the shell in which it is encased,
The love I have for you
Circles ever more closely in and around you,
Until I cannot tell you from that love;

Much as the nut produces the shell
And the shell becomes another nut,
Or so it seems to the chicken
Looking through eggshell in lamplight;
Or prose and the prose writer, himself
Waxing, at some juncture, poetical,
Becomes fuel for the flame
That can never burn its self out,
As long as spirit inhabits the blood
Wherein a pulse in sensed.

More closely, and closer still
Will I ever explore your shores
And central mountain range,
So that I be not estranged
From your very essence,
The which I am blessed by
More intimately, even yet
Than by the marvel that beset me
When first I ventured to inspect thee
On a spectrum from faint glow
To the only growing light I know.

# THE FRESHET

During the freshet, at spring's approach,
Hand me a bowl of wine and I will drink in your spirit.
Sure sore am I crossed and vexed with anguish.
Grant me entrance to transformative possession,
And respite from the absence awaiting her hopeful smile.

Darkness lacerates me with its claws.
Beauty's long awaited dawning, reveal,
While I transcend my cumbrous travail,
A wind untethered from a sail;

To ferry a drowsed and droning bee
From the portico of flower inn,
And tuck her safe and sound
Back in her hive again.

Across the foreground of projected features,
The sketch of a treacherous and lecherous brood
Stepping out of the mist with sticks and stones,
And larger than life with impending doom;
Tromping through the battered gate
With thundering's that make the earth shake.

I don't know how much more I can take!

In the end the plastic figures
Ceremonially execute their maker,

Who arises resurrected,
As is to be expected
In a mythos theologic.

As regards the forces of darkness
And the invincible armies of light,
When you see them in your mind's eye
As you lie awake at night,
Tracing the cat's eye of the moon
Hanging from her neck, at the end of a chain,
She feeds you a line of her soul;

"The inverted breast is as a wooden bowl."

# WEAVING COTTON CANDY

Through the latticed gate of thine established encampment
Come wafted, on wavering banners of titillating breezes,
The perfumes wherewith the tender grasses
Of thy trilling compound are inundated.

Even the insects escaping delirious
From thy delicious orchards
Are like fair smelling brooches
And hair ornaments adorning thy beloveds;
And every one a living testament
Of the consummate care with which
Thou dost beautify the natures thou hast created.

I do not see thee at work.
A flurry of fluttering forest
Dost veil thine ingenious activity;
But all that musically vibrates
And brilliantly radiates, dost bespeak
The cunning artistry of thy glorifying ingenuity.

A company of giddy butterflies
Hath landed, ticklingly, upon me,
As if, I were a burgeoning bush of roses;
And draw from my petaled chalices,
The sumptuous and rejuvenating nectar
Thou hast filled the bottomless well
Of my hallowed heart with;

And each kisses my desirous mouth, at parting,
With nourishing kisses, thou hast destined for me,
As if thou thyself wert delivering them,
Majestic courier of the presence of divinity.

I leave my collection of white garments beneath me,
As rising, I dissolve into the exulting sunlight
Of thy noblizing embraces;
My virgin roots tingling in the animated air
Of thine exhilarating exhalations.

# Theaters

The sky is a theater tonight!
Shooting stars and fireflies
Performing, the parts
Flashing, before my eyes;
And the full, blue moon,
Hymns a coronal tune,
Accompanying, opened wide
The dancers, shuffling to and fro,
Arm in arm, and side by side.

I have a front row seat,
And it happens to me,
As I tap my feet,
I am become a bride;
And my veil is lifted over my head,
As you touch me deep inside;
Nor can I my joy hide,
For my face is all a smile,
Lasting the longest while.

Clouds have come to blot the scene,
But I, already steeped in dream,
Consider another lively show;
Frosted etchings, flakes of snow,
Winter wonders seasoned, so
To give me thrills and make me merry,

Affix my heart with the wings of a fairy;
And it plays the part of mirror moon,
Hymning and humming the self-same tune.

My soul is a theater tonight!
Thoughts and images,
Following a script
Muttered by my sleeping lips;
Dancing as dancers, soft and slow,
Who, slumber's peace, have come to know;
While lines become encoiled,
Embossed on silver foil,
Whereupon, my spirit glows.

# HOME

I come home and change my clothes,
Put on a royal robe and purple,
Remember my chosen place
While looking in God's face,
And move to the center of the circle.

I am only luminous in His light,
And it tickles me to shine so bright,
So I do it every night;
It differs from the light of the sun,
As I am dark, but comely one.

I sit in the branches of His apple tree
And a flaming sword dances before me;
The ark of a mystic moon
Blossoms in full bloom,
And its petals fall around me;

A score of doves arise
To take me by surprise;
They usher, in the wind,
A song writ by Him,
And I dream and sigh;

Somehow the words I knew
Before they let them loose,
And they serve as a reminder
That everything is finer
When it's renewed;

And so, I change my clothes,
Put on a royal robe,
Stand in that chosen place
Where God and I are face to face,
And I call it home.

# Nocturnal Assimilations

Sleep, you ever radical chalice of sacred dream,
How quietly you steal o'er me your poppied wreathe,
Slowly lowering down around my raven tressed crown,
The amulet charmed chain, to nestle on shoulders, enthroned,
That ere I peer below, I have already lost sight and sound,
As gems o'er crust my ears and eyes, like barnacles a ship's sides,
In the bustling dry dock of my mind's eye.

The house fire, like a warm friend, blankets
This babe-like doser, as she slips her mortal coil
For diaphanous threads, stitched by seamstresses of dream,
To fit variegated scenes stage hands and decorators
Carpenter and ornament to dress each out flowering niche,
Thru which the transforming dreamer will streak,
A comet thru the cosmos of sleep.

The trap door clasp swings wide, undone,
While the psychenaut dreamer, liquefied, is funneled
Thru a creeping chasm, where floweth a runnel
Beneath the Pythian priestess of Delphi,
Above, on her tripod, presiding,
The course of the dreamer deciding;
A vein, as it winds thru crystal.

I accompany, as a curious observer
Standing beside a table as server
Bent on waiting hand and foot

The patron come to banquet,
To anticipate her every need,
Describe the flavors of the cuisine
So they intrigue the palate.

Yet, I too am sitting at table,
Double mindedly and doppelganger able
To play the parts of Dante and Virgil,
While Bellerophon keeps a diligent vigil
On winged Pegasus, harnessed with golden bridle,
Narrating the script of an Epistle fashioned of Grecian mythos.

We circle the God, Apollo,
Who, in a platinum hewn alcove,
In conversing with Michelangelo,
Presently contemplating a fresco
Composed of somnambulistic flamingos

Promenading on singular stalks,
Pogo stick-like with pink, flaming tufts;
And we meet Hieronymous Bosch,
Whose vision of paradise, gauche,
Our Milton, he did not share,
Who approaches, as a debonair
The subject matter of creation
In a vacuum Hebrew-Christian
From which the living are residual.

Dream, the ever phantasmical designer,
Is never actually seen, himself;

Although, I intimate the cloudy footprints
By which the Morophean elf climbed to the couch of Iris,
And there, lazes largely sublime,
As she slides on her arched rainbow to and fro the sky;

And she butterfly flits in Zepyrus' stream,
Moonlight glowing thru her cathedral wings,
And hands me her namesake's flower,
With all of its mystical power,
As a key to the Hades sealed memory,
To admit entrance of my companion seeking soul
In the nether world below.

At the threshold, I'm greeted by Persephine,
And she gifts me a little box,
The contents of which are beauty
Which cause a languishing coma
Dispelled by the kiss of Eros,
To initiate the heiros gamos
Of Divinity and humanity;

And with Morpheus, now, I rise,
The two into one entwined;
My eternal thirst slaked,
As up, thru the chasm, I break
From the theater house of dream,
Through the permeable membrane of sleep,
And, in the arms of Dawn, I awaken.

Ancient embalmer of beloved poesy,
Whereas before you did hardly know me,
As if my tongue, cripple winged, had been clipped,
Now both flutter creative utterance
Of a telling dove on grains of the shore,

Who's been to the center of the labyrinth
And held her own 'gainst surly Minotaur.

I return to my everyday affairs,
To the fire, lend aid and care;
The logs so devoutly devoured
Leave only their ash for the air,
Much as my dreams softly slumber,
Until, once again, I go under
And ride the electric chair.

# ORANGE AND GOLD

Orange and gold, you came to me so boldly,
Burning out loud everything in your holding,
And you do it so nobly.

Why is it no one told me; are they all too proud,
Or do they just not know how to voice the sweet serene
Deep within your meaning?

You come to me divine and tip the scale of mind,
To touch upon the soul waiting there for all
Who slip the bonds of time.

I give up my cushioned seat, for the wings upon my feet
Are itching so to rise and take the glorious sky
To its smiling surprise;

And there, I meet the eagle shooting from a cloud,
To twist and turn with seagulls who cast their shadowed shrouds
On surging waves that prowl

And churn the sleeping shore with their pouncing claws,
To sift the sparkling gems and leave them as a hem
Upon a wind that sweeps

Along the curving beach o'er which I wind,
And though before I was blind, now gratefully I see
The beauty meant to be.
Orange and gold, I am as one who is sold
Concerning the life you give to everything that lives;
And so, for you, this poem …

# REACHING BEYOND REALITY

Sword bestrewn, birch wattle
Lumber in the shocked grass;
Tweet seeds impregnate particles of wind
With a lifetime's dreams yet singing;
Pondering tips caress Spanish moss
Coiled around, scarfing a bulging throat.

I'm a wizened druid leaning on a green stick,
Razing cane sparks in the grey gravel,
Smelling of the perfume she wore
When first she adorned this sunlit thicket;
For the birch were knee high then,
And I, a lad weaving daisy chains,
In dirt brown, calf high corduroys,
Glanced up from my pensive looping
To explore her sashay by,
She, who is my mother,
Who now has left her body.

I would build a forest fort
With the white birch
For a make shift cabin,
But I would be too large for its opening,
Nor could I lie comfortably supine
On the floor its walls suspend upon.

But, if I were little, like a cricket,
I could sit at mushroom table

And sip purple pansy tea
While my mother laughed with me,
Leaning into the window
Like a bush of rustling roses
For when after this poem closes.

# FUEL FOR FIRE

It isn't that I don't like snow slanting across my window,
Early morning, waiting for coffee and a little cream to lighten the
sky.
It's just that the snow looks like stars loosed from the fixed empyrean,
And the train barreling through town makes an accompanying
apocalyptic soundtrack.

No, it's not as though I am ill equipped
Or without proper coverings to combat the chill;
My boots and gloves are on the oak bench in the mudroom,
And a scarf the kids gave me hangs on the exercise bike
In the back bedroom vacated some years ago;

And I've still got that old ratty jacket
I stole out of a homeless guy's grocery cart
In the alleyway, that time in Chicago
I found myself without suitable attire and convinced
Newspaper would keep him just as warm.

O, and I have built snowmen on occasion and flapped
A great winged bird and swam a long legged frog
In making hollow graphic impressions of snow angels.

So, its not as if I could be accused of having it in for winter;
Making this entire hullabaloo to persuade you to change your mind
That we might reach a consensus, here at the kitchen table.
It's just that as I've gotten older realization of death ever nearer
Has caused a subtle paranoia to creep into my constitution;

Couple that with failing vision and a host of medicinal supplements
I pop like m and m candies every morning
And you can sort of see, maybe, why I have chosen the snow
To project these feelings onto;
As if each flake were emblematic of psychological issues
I am unconsciously battling; for my Eros has prohibited
My ever curious Psyche from revealing such things to me.

But, if you are familiar with he myth, I have been awakened
By the hot wax droplet and there is nowhere I might hie
To avoid the inevitability of becoming a snow man
Or angel, and then melting, myself.

# TURNING US INTO HIS RESPLENDENT RUBIES

Our Beloved has a cache of resplendent rubies
Hanging from his silken belt and clustered in a burlap pouch

We come with hearts full of longing and as dry as a
Handful of dust to the door of His singing tavern

His cedar door knows the contortions of our figures
Have been chiseled by fruitful labor in His white fields
And opens as if by magical incantation

The light within pours onto porch planks liquid gold
As we wade into the sickle of His open armed invitation

Pressing us close into Himself He gives us His pouch
Drink He says these rubies are the wine of My love

We assume new born incarnations of ourselves
And He tells us as He twirls us to the door
You will do with the wine as you will
And come to know your will as My own

Giving of the wine to all you meet
Until the bottles of your hearts are emptied

Then aimlessly wandering with that eternal thirst of yours
You will arrive miraculously at My door
Over and over again until you are no more
But others of My resplendent rubies

# HORSEHAIR PLASTER PRESENTATION

Molten in the morning,
O, flaming sun, arise;
Opening purple eyelids
To a pink and blue surprise.
Climbing through a window
On soft white clouds I ride,
Which emulate the moon's glow
Till I am by your side.

The dolphin, seal, and walrus
Together join to form
An uroboric circle
To orbit Sister Dawn,
Dancing in a saffron gown
In the arms of the joyous sea;
And she is in the valley now
Beneath a towering mountain's feet.

Silent in the sunlight,
The half inch fibers float;
Invisible in shadow,
Tell me, where'd they go?
I cup my hands to find them,
But they are yet unseen
Then comes a shaft of sun's light
In which they create the scene.

Waking reveler, spellbound,
In this life not a dream
Unfolding mythic moment,
Imagination green?
A winged puer aeternus,
To mine own self I seem;
An image from the Sistine Chapel,
Finally  broken free!

# YOUR IMAGE

Your image kissed my eyes this morning,
Golden and red as the sun of dawn;
How I was blinded by the sight,
And my heart tumbled over
Like a basket of trembling flowers.

Your image caressed my mind this evening,
Purple and black as the sky of twilight;
How I was drawn upward,
And my soul was opened
Like a universe in mourning.

Your image glowed in my spirit this dream time,
White and clear like perceptible purity;
How I was cleansed entirely,
And my life began anew
In the wealth of your mercy.

# Fade Thou Not Away

Alas, sweet dream, prithee, "Fade thou not away",
Knowing full nigh thou wilt;
For the Gordian light of the morning is bright
And songbirds sit singing at my windowsill.
I close my eyes with hushed sighs
And say good-bye to my one true love
Passing over the crest of a hill;
And opening eyes to no surprise
I am here alone and lonely still.

My steed won't eat his barleycorn,
He is all skin and bones.
I hear him calling for his home,
But his eyes are dim and weak be his limbs.
He knows no more the road
To loosen his heavy load,
And no longer the strength to strive
My steed lies down and dies.

My feet they burn, my legs they ache,
And there is no blood in the hearts deep break.
My lips are chapped, my throat is parched,
And I find no words to kindle the spark;
But smarting here from Cupid's dart
Walk about in fits and starts,
Praying for the night to fall,
Transporting me from these prison walls
To the delightful glades of sleep,
Where my beloved our sacred love
Forever vowed to keep

# THE HYPERBOLIC POET'S HUBRIS

O hobby horse, stay the course,
I'll take the thrall in stride;
Wings of wind will lift again,
In the air bare back I'll ride,
The knobby kneed Goddess' surprise.

She knew she could inspire,
But she never knew such pace;
History applauds on the sidelines
While I give eternity chase,
In the knobby kneed Goddess' good grace.

I imagine the knobby kneed Goddess
Shaking her brilliant head to relate,
"Forsooth, it is his destiny and not the hand of fate"

# THROUGH THE CRACK

Feet white and barren over lava black
Fold like blank paper into widening cracks,
That the surf her wild story may impress
With a dove soft hand upon my bare breast.

The sun and the moon couched on backs of wave;
The two eternal children sport and play,
And from these thrones delivered to the shore,
One by one increase in numbers more than
All the stars astronomer's see at night;
And gather each like pearl a grain of sand,
And give them to the wind a loft in flight,
Who spins them in to one embracing band
That circles 'round me like a flaming wheel;
When I run down the beach sparks from my heels
Arise like angels thronging all the sky,
And sing the teardrop songs within my eyes:

How once upon a time in sandy tract,
My sister dear and I stood back to back,
A Platonic egg seen through a cracked shell,
Where the yellow and white of egg are held;
Nor did I know in time through cracks we'd run
And the white turn dim and the yellow dun.

Nor at my back does she stand anymore,
But I am here alone on memory's shore,
A swan who's singing early his last song,
That he may find the place where she has gone;

Resume his place beside her on the wave
And two eternal children sport and play,
Till once again delivered to the shore,
We will be making memories once more.

# FOR A MOMENT

Captured in the fall, angels all,
Wings hung up in a dovecot;
And here, in the winding maze,
I am trying to make my way
On softly padded feet,
Over concrete streets
Which once were paved with air
Lighter than feather or strand of hair,
Binding me close and tight
To the fire I witness burning
Deep within her eyes,
The skies of and night,
To the nest wherein her wings
Awaiting, sing.

I clamber up a chain
Composed of drops of rain,
Held tight in her fist
And swinging in the mist;
Back and forth on her pendulum,
Left, right, left, and up and down I go,
From desert sand to artic snow;
And, for a moment, in tropic zone,
I intimate my home
In the midst of her garden croft,
Where I am no longer alone;
For I am centered on her love,
An egg in the nest of the dove,
Undercover of her singing wings.

# THE CLOCK

I can no longer hear the clock
But I remember, tic toc tic toc
I slipped a cog and cleared a bog
Became a prince who was a frog

Fire grew upon this log
That was but dead wood
Refuse on a heap of no use
One a master builder would choose

And I never had a clue
All that He could do
The perfect spherical
The originator of miracles

Till, as I became one
He shone brighter than the sun
And quickened me to the life
Awaiting second sight

In the way of His truth
All lies they go proof
Cathedral ceilings
Beneath a raised roof

And my soul on feathered wings
She rises high and sings
And the Angels all rejoice
To see such a thing

He handed me the key
To immortality
And He allowed me to be
A part of His eternity

I remember the clock
Tic toc tic toc
And then Time itself is shocked
An uncarved block

# Me-Too and His Lean-To

Me-Too's Lean-To is solid axis,
Readily accessible, favored go to
An opening which Me-Too can lean to
When he needs to
A three sided structure attached to living trees
Whose walls and roof are of loose fitting
And lilting saffron and crimson fabric
A perfect habitat for his rabbit heart

Me-Too's Lean-To is a transformation clamber
And there is a ladder on which he clambers
From dirt brown ground to where stars abound
And like a chameleon he shifts color
From amber to dusk asunder
All the while blushing with wonder

Me-Too's Lean-To he imagines with wings
And he travels the universe in his flying machine
Fast on the heels of mercurial dream
Birthing in bevies' fleet clusters of spark
To accompany him upon his lark
And the Angel aglow in his rabbit heart

You see our Me-Too he needs his Lean-To
For imperfection has led him to sorrows
And though they happened once upon a yesterday
They still feature prominent in his tomorrows
So the universe has provided a way
To gift him a brand new day

And you too can Lean-To Me-Too,
When you are wearied and overladen
For Me-Too is a Helpful Maiden
And can conduct you on a voyage
To help you sort your storage
And unpack the one choicest treasure
By which your life can be joyfully measured
By the beat of a gleeful rabbit heart's feet

All the best, Thumper!!!

# FISHY LEAVES

A leaf can't be a fish.
But, it could be a boat, I guess.
Leaves do not have fins,
Therefore, they cannot swim.
But, they can float in a homemade moat.

It would have to be an evergreen pine,
At least to my mind, to emulate the motion
Of things under the ocean.
But, leaves all tend to sink,
Once they brook beneath the brink.

I guess, if I had a toke or two …
I could conclude with you,
If it be your one sole wish,
That a leaf can be a fish.

# Bloodlines

So much so upon your words I hung,
Like a child fighting sleep;
As if I'd never hear again, from tongue
Whose song, so honey sweet,
Could cull a sun from the dark deep
Of the black unknowing night;
As if a magician with all his magic might
Had made his spell words real,
And the very thing he conjures up
Is the mirror of his promise,
Whose operations, honest,
I could compute them step by step
And the very promise resurrect
When I found my proper audience;
And I could read it on their eyes,
The strain to keep them opened up,
While I caressed the strings of my heart's own lute
In memory of you,
In an endless stream of love,
And the power of the living truth:
That together we are one.

www.ingramcontent.com/pod-product-compliance
Lightning Source LLC
Chambersburg PA
CBHW021119130626
46554CB00002B/771